LEVEL
II

McMaster
English

Contents

01

The Solar System

1 The Solar System

I Write the key words of the passage.

Our solar system has the Sun, nine planets, and their moons. The centre of the solar system is the Sun. The closest planet to the Sun is Mercury. Pluto is the farthest and smallest planet. All the planets in our solar system orbit around the Sun.

_____

II Write the topic sentence of the passage.

Meteor showers can be predicted. For instance, we can predict a meteor shower from July 25th through August 18th. It is called Preseid meteor shower. Meteor showers repeat every year when the Earth passes through the orbit of comets. During meteor

showers, thousands of meteors make long and thin lines across the sky.

_____

Read the passage and answer questions.

Saturn is the sixth planet from the Sun. Saturn is famous for its thousands of beautiful shiny rings. Saturn's rings are bigger and brighter than any other planet's rings.

Scientists have been studying Saturn's rings. They discovered that the particles in Saturn's rings are ice and rock. How did the ring form? The origin of the rings of Saturn is still unknown. Some scientists believe that a moon of Saturn broke into pieces and formed the rings around Saturn.

1. What is the main topic of the passage?
   a. Saturn and other planets
   b. Saturn and the Sun
   c. Saturn's moons
   d. Saturn's rings

2. Which of the following is true about Saturn's rings?
   a. They are darker than other planet's rings.
   b. They are one of the Saturn's moons.
   c. Scientists are still studying how they are formed.
   d. They are getting smaller.

IV Read the passage and answer questions.

Comets are sometimes called "dirty snowballs" because they are made of ice and dust. If you mix some dirt, stones, and water together, then freeze them, you would have a miniature of a comet.

Comets move through the solar system in long, narrow orbits. Only a few comets come close to the Sun. When they approach the Sun, the Sun heats and melts them. The comet's ice turns into gas and dust to make a long tail. The comet shows its grand tail across the sky.

1. What is the best title for the passage?
   a. What are comets?
   b. Who found comets?
   c. When did comets form?
   d. How do comets travel?

2. What makes a comet visible?
   a. Frozen masses of ice and dust
   b. Dirt and water
   c. Particles from the Sun
   d. Heated gas and dust

V Read the passage and answer questions.

The Sun is the largest object in our solar system. Its diameter is about 1.4 million kilometers. That is 109 times the diameter of the Earth. It contains more than 99.8% of the total mass of our solar system.

The Sun is a huge ball of flaming gas. It is composed of about 70% hydrogen and 28% helium. The Sun uses hydrogen as a fuel to make heat and light energy. Therefore, the composition of gases changes slowly over time in its core.

1. What is the main idea of paragraph 1?
    a. The Sun is the biggest object in the universe.
    b. The Sun is the largest star in our solar system.
    c. The Sun is the only star in the universe.
    d. The size of the Sun is not known.

2. What is the Sun mostly composed of?
    a. Hydrogen
    b. Helium
    c. Water
    d. Helium and water

Actual Mini *TOEFL*

Until the beginning of the 17th century, only eight objects including the Sun and the Moon were known in the universe. Europeans thought that the Earth was the at the center and other bodies *revolved* around it.

In 1610 Galileo first turned a telescope on the heavens and the universe. He discovered Saturn and its rings. By the end of the 17th century, Copernicus' theory was widely accepted. He insisted that the Sun was at the center of our solar system and the Earth orbited the Sun.

The number of objects discovered in the solar system *increased* dramatically in the 19th century. Hundreds of asteroids and the eighth planet Neptune were discovered.

1. **What is the main topic of the passage?**
   a. The number of objects in the solar system
   b. Many kinds of objects in the solar system
   c. The history of the solar system discovery
   d. The history of the universe

2. **What did Europeans think of the Earth in the 16th century?**

    a. It is the biggest object in the universe.

    b. It is the center of the universe.

    c. It is the oldest object in the universe.

    d. It is the origin of the u inverse.

3. **When was Neptune first discovered?**

    a. In the 16th century

    b. In the 17th century

    c. In the 18th century

    d. In the 19th century

4. **The word "revolved" in the passage is closest in meaning to**

    a. revived

    b. orbited

    c. came

    d. changed

5. **The word "increased" in the passage is opposite in meaning to**

    a. influenced

    b. advised

    c. reduced

    d. reviewed

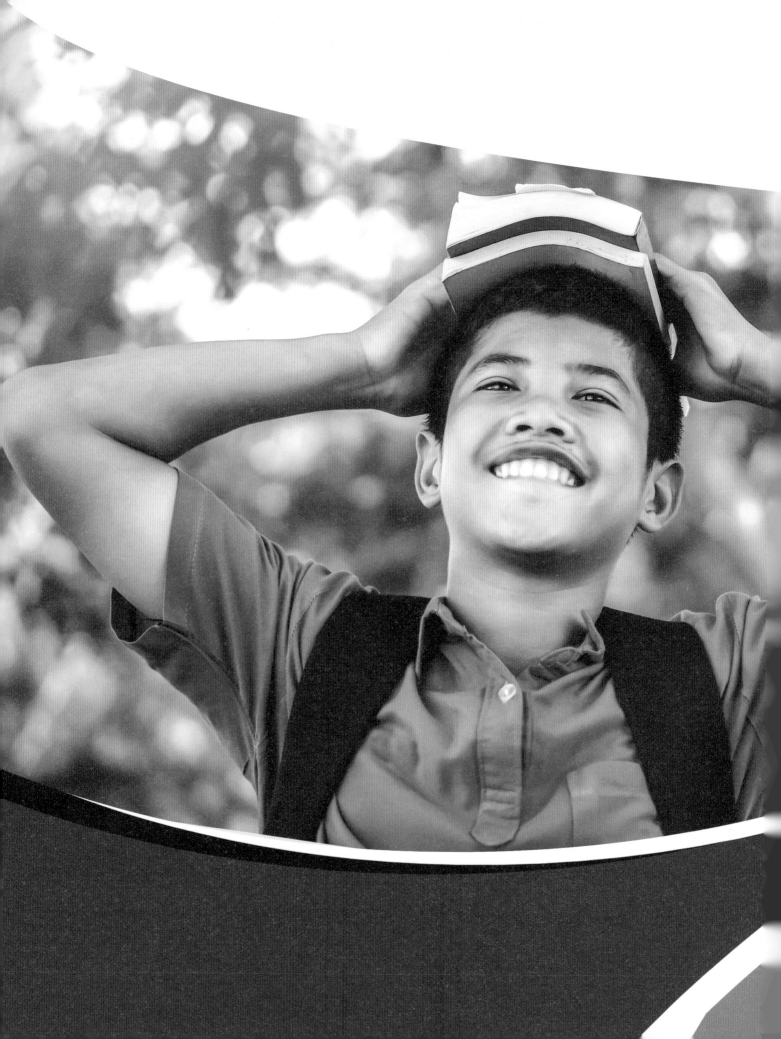

02

Wars and Revolutions

2 Wars and Revolutions

I Write the key words of the passage.

During World War II Germany, Italy, and Japan comprised the Axis Powers. The war began when Germany invaded Poland in 1939. It ended on August 15, 1945 after the United States dropped atomic bombs on Hiroshima and Nagasaki in Japan.

_____

II Write the topic sentence of the passage.

The Revolutionary War was fought to gain American independence. America at the time were 13 colonies under the rule of Great Britain. Britain asked Americans to pay more taxes. It caused Americans to insist on their independence.

_____

Ⅲ **Read the passage and answer questions.**

Europe was divided into two groups in World War I. One alliance connected Germany and Austria-Hungary. It was called Central Powers. The other alliance connected France  and Britain to Russia and it was called Allied Powers.

In 1914 Austria-Hungary declared war and the Great War began. The United States joined the war in 1917 after Germany killed 128 Americans. American troops and supplies helped end the war. The Treaty of Versailles was signed in 1919 and the terrible war ended. During this war, millions of men died.

1. **What is the main topic of the passage?**
   a. The cause of World War I
   b. The result of World War I
   c. A summary of World War I
   d. Two Powers in Europe

2. **What made the United States join the war?**
   a. Many Americans lived in Europe.
   b. Many Americans were killed by Germany.
   c. The United States was allied with Austria-Hungary.
   d. Many Americans had a war against Russia.

IV Read the passage and answer questions.

When Britain left India in 1947, India found its independence. After World War II, Pakistan separated from India because of the question of religion. India was primarily made up of Muslims. Wars between the two countries continued and many people died. Millions of people moved to India or Pakistan according to their faith.

Conflicts between the Hindus and the Muslims are still a problem. The Muslims in northwestern India desire independence. Big and small wars at their borders have not stopped.

1. What is the main idea of the passage?
   a. India and Pakistan were divided by their belief.
   b. Britain separated India from Pakistan.
   c. India was independent from Britain.
   d. Most Indians are Hindus.

2. Which country did most of the Muslims move to?
   a. India
   b. Pakistan
   c. Britain
   d. Nepal

Actual Mini *TOEFL*

Revolution means a complete change in the way of doing things. The Industrial Revolution change the way goods were made. Before the 1700s, people made clothes, baskets, and furniture by hand at home. The steam engine, invented by James Watt, made mass production possible. His steam engine resulted in other inventions. Trains, nicknamed "Iron Horse," steam boats, and other machines were invented and used in Europe.

The Industrial Revolution began in Britain and it spread to France, Germany, and America. As industries in those countries grew rapidly, they needed more labor for factories and markets for products. To meet their needs, they explored new land and invaded other countries. The revolution created political changes in the world.

1. **What is the main topic of the passage?**
   a. The inventor, James Watt
   b. Inventions in the world
   c. Industrial growth in Europe
   d. Industrial Revolution

2. **What is the main idea of paragraph 2?**

   a. The Industrial Revolution began in Britain.

   b. The Industrial Revolution spread to many countries.

   c. A few countries in Europe invaded other countries.

   d. The Industrial Revolution created changes in the world.

3. **How did people in 1680 make clothes?**

   a. By hand

   b. With machines

   c. In factories

   d. With skins from animal

4. Where did the Industrial Revolution begin?

   a. In Britain

   b. In France

   c. In Germany

   d. In America

5. The word "rapidly" in the passage is closest in meaning to

   a. slowly

   b. partly

   c. quickly

   e. easily

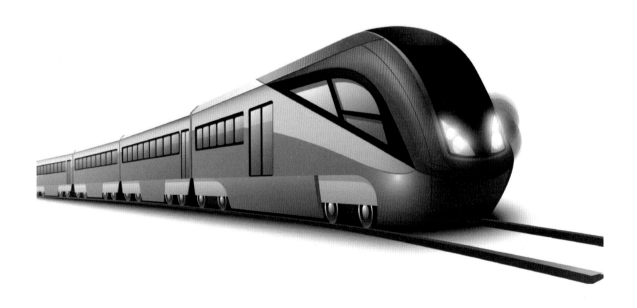

03

Film and Play

3 Film and Play

I Write the key words of the passage.

Actors learn their lines and their movements by heart. A director tells them how to move and how to say their lines. They wear special clothes for the play. They perform the play for an audience. The audience cheers as they take a bow. Actors love to hear the sound of the applause when the play is over.

II Write the topic sentence of the passage.

Movies have changed over the past centuries. The earliest films ran only 10 minutes and showed simple actions. The camera was used in a fixed position.  Modern films have long and complex stories. The director apply newer technology and special effects to their movies. Especially computers play important roles in making films.

III Read the passage and answer questions.

Woody Allen is one of the most well-known and respected people in the film industry. He is a writer, screenwriter, director, actor, musician, and producer. He has been working in movies for over 30 years.

He combined the features of drama with those of comedy. His films cover a wide variety of genres, from documentaries to comedies and from theatre-style dramas to musicals. His films are entertaining and humorous. They make people consider important questions. Woody Allen always gives his audience a film well worth their time and money.

1. **What is the best title of the passage?**
   a. Woody Allen's career and films
   b. Woody Allen, a famous screenwriter
   c. Woody Allen, a famous actor
   d. Woody Allen's life

2. **Which of the following is not a genre that Woody Allen's film covers?**
   a. Comedy
   b. Documentary
   c. Musical
   d. Animation

IV Read the passage and answer questions.

The theatre of old times was quite different from the theatre we see today. The theatre originated in the cultures of dancing in primitive societies. Primitive people danced in the theatre to please supernatural beings. They thought that the supernatural beings controlled their lives.

They also danced to get rid of evil spirits. They believed that evil spirits made diseases. The actors doing the dances wore the masks that looked like evil spirits. And they wore the costumes made of animal skins or plants.

1. What is the main topic of the passage?
    a. The dancing of primitive societies
    b. Supernatural beings
    c. The theatre's origin
    d. Today's theatre

2. What did the actors wear when they danced?
    a. Masks that looked like evil spirits
    b. Costumes that looked liked animals
    c. Masks that were made of animal skins
    d. Costumes that had supernatural powers

Actual Mini TOEFL

The theatre in Asia is mostly symbolic. The actors *performing* in Asian theatre wear masks or artificial makeup. An actor wearing a mask represents a character. If an actor has a whip in his hand, it represents a man on horseback. Western theatre is more realistic. The actors play exactly who the characters are and what they are doing in the theatre. They don't wear masks and they ride real horses, if possible.

There is an Asian theatre that some Western audiences are familiar with. It is the Kabuki theatre in Japan. Kabuki is a kind of Japanese drama. The Kabuki stage extends into the audience and to the back of the auditorium. And the theatre has a revolving stage.

1. What is the main topic of the passage?
    a. Western theatre
    b. Asian theatre
    c. Japanese theatre
    d. Western theatre and Asian theatre

2. **What is Kabuki?**

    a. Western theatre

    b. Japanese theatre

    c. Japanese drama

    d. Japanese actor

3. **What is true about Western theatre?**

    a. It is realistic.

    b. The actor in the theatre wears heavy makeup.

    c. The actor in the theatre wears a mask.

    d. It is symbolic.

4. Which of the following is not true about the Kabuki theatre?

    a. It has a revolving stage.

    b. The Kabuki stage extends to the back of auditorium.

    c. It is a kind of Western theatre.

    d. Some Western audiences are familiar with it.

5. The word "performing" in the passage is closest in meaning to

    a. revolving

    b. playing

    c. walking

    d. standing

04

The Great People

4 The Great People

I Write the words that "He" refers to.

Alexander the Great was only 20 years old, when he became a king. His life ended at the age of 33. Even though his life was short, he changed the world history forever. _He_ spread Hellenism throughout the Middle East and into Asia. He set the stage for the establishment of the Roman Empire.

_____

II Write the word that is closest in meaning to "freedom."

When Benjamin Franklin was young, the American colonies were ruled by England. The Americans went to war for their _freedom_. During the war, he  went to Europe to represent Americans. He signed the Declaration of Independence. He also contributed to peace with England after the country won its independence. He is remembered as the best diplomat.

_____

III Read the passage and answer questions.

Martin Luther King. Jr. was born in Atlanta on January 15, 1929. His grandfather and father were pastors of a church. He was influenced by Mahatma Gandhi who used nonviolence as a method of social change. _He_ played a great role in getting African American's civil rights in the Untied States.

In his time, black people could not ride with white people on the same bus. It was Montgomery's policy on buses. King and other civil rights activists _refused_ to follow the policy. They led the campaign and were able to change the world at last.

1. What does the word "He" in the passage refer to?
   a. Mahatma Gandhi
   b. Black people
   c. Civil rights activist
   d. Martin Luther King. Jr.

2. The word "refused" in the passage is opposite in meaning to
   a. reduced   b. repeated
   c. accepted   d. respected

IV Read the passage and answer questions.

Hellen Keller was no more than two years old when she became blind and deaf. It happened to her suddenly because of a high fever. As she grew up, she realized that she could not understand what other people said.

But she discovered that words were related to things. She *tried* to learn language. Her teacher spelled words on her hand. Then *she* could learn what her teacher spelled. She had a hunger to express her thoughts and feelings. Helen Keller could neither hear nor see but she lectured all over America, raising funds for the blind.

1. What does the word "she" in the passage refer to?
   a. the blind
   b. Helen Keller
   c. other people
   d. Helen Keller's teacher

2. What is the word "tried" in the passage closest in meaning to?
   a. happened
   b. liked
   c. needed
   d. attempted

V Read the passage and answer questions.

The first aircraft, the Wright Flyer, was made of wood and fabric. *It* was invented and built by Wilbur and Orville Wright. The Wright brothers used the facilities of their bicycle shop in Ohio to construct an aircraft.

They began experiment with their kite in 1899. They tried over and over to solve the basic problems of mechanical flight.

On December 17, 1903, the Wright Flyer surprised the world. The power-driven airplane flew near Kitty Hawk, North Carolina on that day. Of their four flights, the one by Wilbur covered 260 meters and *lasted* 59 seconds.

1. The word "It" in the passage refers to
   a. Their bicycle
   b. Fabric
   c. The Wright Flyer
   d. Ohio

2. The word "lasted" in the passage is opposite in meaning to
   a. stopped
   b. went
   c. continued
   d. ran

Actual Mini *TOEFL*

Mother Teresa is **_well known_** for the work she did for other people. She was born in Albania but she spent most of her life India.

She helped **_sick_** people. She fed hungry people. She provided the places to live for homeless people. She took care of children with no families. All the people she helped were very, very poor.

Mother Teresa won many awards. In 1979 she was awarded the Nobel Prize. She used the award money to help poor people as she spent her whole life working for **_them_**. On September 5, 1997, people all over the world mounted over her death. Now other nuns and volunteers take over her work to help poor people.

1. **What is the main idea of the passage?**
   a. Mother Teresa was famous around the world.
   b. Mother Teresa won the Nobel Peace Prize.
   c. Mother Teresa spent her whole life helping poor people.
   d. Mother Teresa's work will continue.

2. What does the word "them" in the passage refer to?

   a. Mother Teresa

   b. other nuns

   c. poor people

   d. volunteers

3. The phrase "well known" in the passage is closest in meaning to

   a. famous

   b. bright

   c. smart

   d. helpful

4. What did Mother Teresa do with the award money?

   a. She saved it for her.

   b. She spent it for her family.

   c. She paid for volunteers.

   d. She spent it helping the poor.

5. The word "sick" in the passage is opposite in meaning to

   a. hungry

   b. healthy

   c. tired

   d. angry

05

Places and Neighbors

5 Places and Neighbors

I Write the word that "It" refers to.

Iraq is a country in Asia. Its population is about 24,700,000. About 95% of the population is Muslim. Its capital is Baghdad. Four different languages are spoken in the nation. Its chief crops are wheat, barley, rice, vegetable, and cotton. _**It**_ has a large amount of oil reserve. Oil is the basis of the economy in Iraq.

_____

II Write the word that is opposite in meaning to "largest."

Lake Baikal is in the part of Russia called Siberia. It is known as the deepest lake on the earth. The lake is more than a mile in depth. It is also the third _**largest**_ lake in Asia and the largest freshwater lake in Europe and Asia.

_____

III Read the passage and answer questions.

Olivehurst is a small town in Northern California in the United States. In the beginning of 1997 the town had its worst flood in more than a hundred years. It was caused by rain and melting snow. All of the people in Olivehurst had to leave their homes. Many had to move into shelters.

The flood destroyed the city. When the villagers returned the home, *they* found their houses covered with mud. They cleaned up their houses and worked hard to rebuild the town. The town survived the flood, but their lives would never be the same.

1. What does the word "they" in the passage refer to?
   a. Olivehurst
   b. shelters
   c. the villagers
   d. the houses

2. The word "melting" in the passage is opposite in meaning to
   a. starting
   b. falling
   c. heating
   d. freezing

IV Read the passage and answer questions.

The Isle of Eigg lies just off the west coast of Scotland. More than 500 people had homes on this island.

However, the island always belonged to other people who did not live there. The last owner was a German artist. As a matter of fact, *he* wanted to sell the island.

The islanders decided to buy the island themselves! The farmers, shepherds, and the fishermen on the island started to raise money. They soon set up a Web site and asked people around the world for donations. More than 5,000 people helped the islanders. They were able to raise 2.5 million dollars, enough to buy their island.

1. The word "he" in the passage refers to

    a. a German artist

    b. an islander

    c. a farmer

    d. a fisherman

2. What is the word "raise" in the passage closest in meaning to

    a. buy   b. lend

    c. collect   d. sell

V Read the passage and answer questions.

Hong Kong is made up of the Kow Loon Peninsula on the mainland of China and more than 230 islands.

The main island is Hong Kong Island and it lies at the south of the peninsula. It has 6.7 million residents and most of them are Chinese

Hong Kong was _ruled_ by Britain for 155 years. It has been ruled by the China since July 1, 1997. Even though Hong Kong is a part of China, _it_ is a special region. Britain wants the place to remain a successful trade centre for the world. China hopes that its economy will benefit from Hong Kong.

1. What does the word "it" in the passage refer to?
   a. Britain
   b. Hong Kong
   c. China
   d. Kow Loon Peninsula

2. The world "ruled" in the passage is closest in meaning to
   a. made   b. built
   c. continued   d. controlled

Actual Mini TOEFL

The highest mountain in the world is well known to people. It is Mount Everest measured 8,848 meters high. What is the lowest place on the earth? It is the Dead Sea on the border between Israel and  Jordan. It is about 408 meters below the sea level.

The height of land or mountain is measured from sea level to its top. If we add together the height _above_ sea level and the depth below sea level, the highest point on the earth is Mauna Kea. It means "White Mountain". _It_ is an inactive volcano on the beautiful island of Hawaii. Mauna Kea measures about 9,800 meters from its base on the ocean floor to its top. It is 1,000 meters higher than Mount Everest.

1. **What is the main topic of the passage?**
   a. The highest mountain on the earth
   b. How to measure the height of mountain or land
   c. The lowest place on the earth
   d. The most well-known places on the earth

2. The word "It" in the passage refers to

   a. Mauna Kea

   b. Mount Everest

   c. Dead Sea

   d. Hawaii

3. The word "above" in the passage is opposite in meaning to

   a. high

   b. low

   c. below

   d. deep

4. How is the height of Mount Everest measured?

   a. From its base on the ocean floor to its top

   b. From sea level to its top

   c. From a point below sea level to its top

   d. From a point above sea level to its top

5. How height is Mauna Kea from its base on the ocean floor to its top?

   a. 8,848 meters

   b. 408 meters

   c. 1,000 meters

   d. 9,800 meters

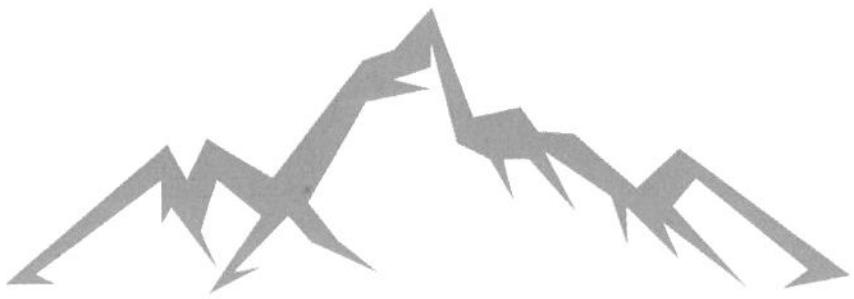

06

American History

6 American History

I Underline the words that "one" refers to and write them.

Samuel Johnson wrote the first English dictionary in 1755. In America, Noah Webster wrote the most famous **_one_** in 1828. It has been updated many times.

_____

_____

II Underline the word that is closest in meaning to "president" and write it.

Abraham Lincoln was the sixteenth **_president_** of America. He helped slaves get freedom. He was a good leader and is still respected by many Americans.

IN THIS TEMPLE
AS IN THE HEARTS OF THE PEOPLE
FOR WHOM HE SAVED THE UNION
THE MEMORY OF ABRAHAM LINCOLN
IS ENSHRINED FOREVER

_____

III Read the passage and answer questions.

After the war was over, America won independence from Britain. People wanted to build a new **_nation_** and they needed a president.

During the war, many people admired George Washington. They thought **_he_** would rule over the country fairly. So he was elected as the first president of America. And Americans named the national capital after Washington.

1. The word "he" in the passage refers to

    a. war

    b. George Washington

    c. people

    d. Britain

2. The word "nation" in the passage is closest in meaning to

    a. city

    b. farm

    c. country

    d. town

IV Read the passage and answer questions.

The American flag is called "Stars and Stripes." A star on the flag means a state of the nation. **_It_** had only thirteen stars in 1777. As time **_passed_**, some stars were added for new states.

After Hawaii became the fiftieth state in 1959, it had fifty stars. And the flag became the official flag of the United States.

1. The word "It" in the passage refers to

    a. American flag

    b. Star

    c. Stripe

    d. State

2. The word "passed" in the passage is closest in meaning to

    a. had

    b. added

    c. went by

    d. needed

Actual Mini *TOEFL*

Thousands of people immigrated to America in the late 19th century. Most of them came from southern and eastern Europe.

American people didn't like the immigrants. **_They_** thought that the newcomers took their jobs. Moreover, the immigrants' religion was different from Americans'. So they could not live in harmony.

Finally, America made a new law to limit immigration. Because of this **_law_**, much fewer people came into America.

1. What is the main topic of the passage?

   a. The history of American immigration

   b. The history of American law

   c. The number of immigrants into America

   d. The immigrants' religion

2. The word "They" in the passage refers to

   a. Immigrants

   b. American people

   c. Jobs

   d. Newcomers

3. The word "law" in the passage is closest in meaning to

   a. law

   b. note

   c. book

   d. rule

07
Music

7 Music

I Write the word that "themselves" refers to.

Music has always played an important role in culture. In early societies music was the most important means of remembering myths of gods and deeds of powerful people. Today, people continue to use music to define *themselves* and celebrate moments of their lives.

_____

II Write the word that is closest in meaning to "remove".

America has many patriotic war songs. Many of these songs were written during World Wars. When the song is sung, people stand up and *remove* their hats. This shows respect for those who served their country.

_____

III Read the passage and answer questions.

Ragtime was an early form of jazz. It was developed by African-American pianists. From the 1890s to about 1915, _**this music**_ became popular in America.

Scott Joplin was a major composer and _**performer**_ of ragtime. He called himself "King of Ragtime writers". His great work is *the Maple Leaf Rag*.
Another well known piece is *Entertainer* using in the film, *the Sting*. He devoted his life making ragtime an important part of American music.

1. The words "this music" in the passage refers to
    a. ragtime
    b. jazz
    c. sheet music
    d. working music

2. The word "performer" in the passage is closest in meaning to
    a. director
    b. writer
    c. painter
    d. player

IV Read the passage and answer questions.

The harp has about 45 strings stretched across its triangular frame. A harpist plays the harp and makes beautiful sounds. Making harp as well as playing the harp is also an art.

George Lyon and Patrick Healy started making harp back in 1864. At the time, Americans imported harps from Europe. But *they* could not withstand the different climate. Lyon & Healy harps can be *found* in symphonies everywhere. The company makes 70 percent of the world's harps. Their custom-made harp costs as much as $28,000.

1. The word "they" in the passage refers to
    a. harpists
    b. Lyon and Healy
    c. imported harps
    d. Lyon & Healy harps

2. The word "found" in the passage is closest in meaning to
    a. built
    b. made
    c. seen
    d. lost

V Read the passage and answer questions.

Every song of Native American is unique, but most of the songs *follow* almost the same format. Their songs consist of four parts: the lead, second, chorus, and ending.

The lead is the first part of a song. The lead singer sings it to introduce the song. *He* does not tell what they are about to sing. The second is a repeat of the lead by the rest of singers. The chorus is the part that carries the main theme of the song. All the singers sing together.

1. The word "follow" in the passage is opposite in meaning to
   a. prepare
   b. precede
   c. part
   d. change

2. What does the word "He" in the passage refers to
   a. The lead singer
   b. The second singer
   c. The chorus singer
   d. A Native American

Actual Mini *TOEFL*

The drum is essential to many ceremonies called "pow wow" in North America. Native Americans believe that the sound of drum stands for the rhythm of life and the pulse of human being.

The instrument drum is made of wood and rawhide. Today, cowhide is usually used although buffalo hide is much better. The average size of the drum is 65 centimetres in diameter. The *sticks* used to strike the drum are thin rods with a leather-head. There are usually about 10 singers around the drum. There are seven or eight men and two or three women. *They* have to sing many songs without repeating even a single song during a pow wow.

1. **What is the main topic of this passage?**
    a. How to play the drum
    b. How to make the drum
    c. The drum used in North America
    d. The drum in the orchestra

2. **What does the word "They" in the passage refers to**

    a. Many ceremonies

    b. The instruments

    c. The singers around the drum

    d. Many drums

3. **The word "sticks" in the passage is the closest in meaning to**

    a. singers

    b. rawhide

    c. drums

    d. rods

4. **What is used in making the drum?**

    a. Steel and wood

    b. Wood and cloth

    c. Cloth and rawhide

    d. Wood and cowhide

5. **How many singers make up the drum?**

    a. Two or three

    b. Ten

    c. Eighteen

    d. More than twenty

08

Natural
Disaster

8 Natural Disaster

I **Underline the sentence that is a clue to the question and write the answer in English.**

Disaster is defined as an accident causing widespread destruction, worries, and pains. Natural disaster includes tornadoes, hurricanes, earthquakes, and volcanoes. They kill people and damage the place where people live. These days most of the natural disasters occur because of environmental pollution.

What causes most of the natural disasters today?

_____

II **Correct the following sentence according to the passage.**

More than 100 people in the United States die from lightning each year. That is more than the number killed by both hurricanes and tornadoes.

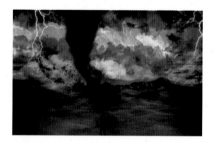

Lightning often occurs during a thunderstorm. It may strike people and severely hurt them in just a few seconds.

A hurricane causes more people to die than lightning does.

_____

III Read the passage and answer questions.

Tornadoes are the most violent phenomenon on the planet. They come with strong winds of 200-300 miles per an hour. Whenever a tornado is warned, and it is threatening, people must follow certain instructions.

In homes or small buildings, it is good to go to the basement. Wrapping the body in overcoats or blankets can protect a person from flying objects. People also should stay away from walls, crouch down and cover their heads. Most death occur in cars or mobile homes. If anyone is in either of these places, he or she should leave them and go to safe shelter.

1. Where is the best place to hide in case of a tornado?
     a. In a basement
     b. In a closet
     c. In a mobile home
     d. In a car

2. All of the following are instructions to follow during tornados except
     a. Keep away from walls
     b. Move to the roof of a house
     c. Leave the cars or mobile homes
     d. Wrap the body in blankets

IV Read the passage and answer questions.

Cyclone, typhoon, and willy-willy are names that are given to hurricanes in different parts of the world. Hurricanes are violent tropical ocean storms with strong winds. The winds at the centre of the hurricane can move at a speed of up to 250 kilometers an hour.

Hurricanes are a danger to people on land as well as to sailors at sea. Hurricanes destroy crops, buildings, bridges, and roads. They make millions of people homeless and kill many people every year. The buildup of water at a storms center can drown a coast and wash away the villages near a coast.

1. Which of the following is true about hurricanes?

    a. They are threatening only at sea.

    b. Many people lose their homes because of them.

    c. They are not strong enough to destroy buildings.

    d. Typhoons are more violent than hurricanes.

2. All of the following mean the same thing except

    a. Cyclone

    b. Willy-willy

    c. Tornado

    d. Typhoon

V Read the passage and answer questions.

The most fearful thing about volcanoes is their explosive eruptions. More than 500 volcanoes have erupted on the earth's surface since ancient times.

A mantle of molten rock covers the earth's core. It constantly rises, cools and sinks. Very high pressure builds up beneath the ground. The endless shaking splits the surface into rocky plates. Like a shaken bottle of soda, magma erupts out the top in the form of lava. Sometimes the eruption is sudden and violent. At other times, the eruption is relatively slow and quiet. The lava flows down like thick honey.

1. According to the passage, what is the earth's core covered with?
   a. Rocky plate
   b. Lava
   c. Magma
   d. Mantle

2. Which of the following is not true about volcanoes?
   a. Volcanoes have erupted since ancient times.
   b. The eruption is always sudden.
   c. Magma erupts in the form of lava.
   d. The lava flows like honey.

Actual Mini TOEFL

Earthquakes occur suddenly and **_destroy_** everything on the ground. The ground cracks during an earthquake and it buries habitats below the ground. Over the centuries people have made various efforts

to predict the earthquakes. Scientist have observed animal behaviours and physical and chemical changes above and below the ground. **_They_** have studied periods between earthquakes. In the early 1980s, some scientists measured ground motion. In 1993 a major earthquake could be predicted.

Earthquakes still happen around the world. The countries that are prone to earthquakes have upgraded their buildings. Japan has spent a lot of money to avoid damage from earthquakes.

1. **What is the main topic of the passage?**

    a. Human's efforts to protect against earthquakes

    b. Earthquakes and animal behaviours

    c. Destruction by earthquakes

    d. Scientists who study earthquakes

2. The word "They" in the passage refer to

    a. People

    b. Scientists

    c. Earthquakes

    d. Animals

3. The word "destroy" in the passage is closest in meaning to

    a. build

    b. break

    c. pull

    d. push

4. Which of the following have the scientists not done to predict earthquakes?

    a. They have observed animal behaviours.

    b. They have studied periods between earthquakes.

    c. They have observed physical change above the ground.

    d. They have observed chemical change in animal bodies.

5. According to the passage, when did scientists predict a major earthquake?

    a. In 1970s

    b. In 1980s

    c. In 1990s

    d. In 2000s

09

Philosophy

9 Philosophy

I. Underline the sentence that is a clue to the question and write the answer in English.

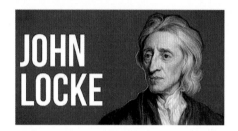

JOHN LOCKE

John Locke was an English philosopher. He was born on August 29, 1632. He studied medicine and science at school but he hadn't a special interest in philosophy. In 1671, Locke began to write his greatest work. It took twenty years to complete the book. It was a book on understanding humans.

When did Locke finish his greatest work?

_____

II. Correct the following sentence according to the passage.

Teenagers are really interested in philosophy. It is the great question that people have been asking for thousands of years. For example, they ask "What is right and what is wrong?" "Can people choose their actions or are they all decided beforehand by fate?" "How does the world get here?"

Young people are not interested in philosophy.

_____

Ⅲ **Read the passage and answer questions.**

Ancient Greek philosophy was developed by three famous philosophers. They are Socrates, Plato, and Aristotle. They all lived in Athens in Ancient Greece.

Socrates was a teacher of Plato. After Socrates was killed, Plato wrote down his own ideas and founded a school called the Academy. Aristotle studied under Plato and wrote many dialogues at the Academy. He also tutored Alexander the Great and opened his own school. They taught important ways of thinking about the world to people in their time and in the following periods.

1. **Who wrote down Socrates' idea?**
   a. Socrates
   b. Plato
   c. Aristotle
   d. A common Greek

2. **According to the passage, which of the following is not true?**
   a. Socrates lived in Athens.
   b. Plato was Socrates's student.
   c. Aristotle opened a school before Plato.
   d. Socrates taught people how to think.

IV Read the passage and answer questions.

Philosophers have asked many questions on human nature such as "Is human nature basically good?" "Is it basically evil?" "Do the circumstances change human nature?"

Many philosophers think that human nature is basically bad. It means that men and women will do something wrong instead of something right without laws or education. They do things that are wrong naturally. Philosophers say people should struggle and try hard to do the right thing. But the question, "What is right?" is not easily answered by people even if they try to do the right thing.

1. According to the passage, what do many philosophers think of human nature?
   a. It is basically good.
   b. It is basically bad.
   c. Humans do the right thing without education.
   d. Humans do the right thing naturally.

2. Which of the following is not true?
   a. People basically know what is right.
   b. People must try to do the right thing.
   c. Laws help people do the right thing.
   d. Philosophers have studied human nature.

V Read the passage and answer questions.

Socrates was born in Athens in 469 BC. He was not from a wealthy family. It is said that his father was a stone-carver. Socrates himself also worked on stones. In his later  years, he married Xanthippe who is known as a bad wife.

When he was in his forties, he began to think about the world around himself. He tried to answer serious questions like "What is wisdom?" "What is beauty?" and "What is right conduct?" He went around Athens and asked these questions of the people he met. He spent his time discussing virtue and justice whenever the citizens congregated.

1. When did Socrates begin to think about the world?
   a. When he was born.
   b. When he was young.
   c. When he was sick.
   d. When he was in his forties.

2. Which of the following is not true about Socrates?
   a. He was not rich when he was young.
   b. He discussed religion.
   c. He worked on stones.
   d. He lived in Athens.

Actual Mini TOEFL

Philosophy means the love of wisdom. **_It_** is related to religion, science, and mathematics. All of these are subjects that have fascinated people for centuries.

Philosophers try to answer the questions about how people should behave. They ask "Is there such a thing as right or wrong? and "How can you tell what is right and what is wrong?" We should call this ethics. Other philosophers are more interested in how the world works and ask "Is there a such a thing as _fate_?" Some philosophers are more interested in the natural world than they are in people. "Where did the world come from? They ask.

1. **What is the main topic of the passage?**

   a. The history of the philosophy

   b. The relations between philosophy and religion

   c. Philosophers' question

   d. The answers for the questions

2. What does the word "It" in the passage refer to
    a. Religion
    b. Mathematics
    c. Wisdom
    d. Philosophy

3. The word "fate" in the passage is closest in meaning to
    a. destiny
    b. future
    c. reality
    d. nature

4. According to the passage, what does the word philosophy mean?
    a. Beauty of human
    b. Power of religion
    c. Order of nature
    d. Love of wisdom

5. All of the following are the philosophers' questions except
    a. What is right?
    b. Where is my partner?
    c. How is the world made?
    d. What is my fate?

10 Art

10 Art

I Underline the sentence that is a clue to the question and write the answer in English.

From ancient wall painting in caves to modern art, people have used their imagination to create an art. Ancient Egyptians discovered that a reed could be used as a brush. They changed their style of an art form developed all over the world. These include Abstract art, Naturalism, Expressionism, and Romanticism.

What did ancient Egyptians use as a brush?

_____

II Correct the following sentence according to the passage.

A line is the connection between two or more points. Artist use lines to make shapes and symbols. Lines can be thick, curved, straight, broken, and wavy. Mixed and connected lines make styles and images and express feelings.

Writers use lines to express their feelings.

_____

III Read the passage and answer questions.

Artists use various techniques in their pictures. To pull viewers in their pictures, artist use the technique called linear perspective. Linear perspective is a mathematical technique for creating the illusion of space and distance on a flat

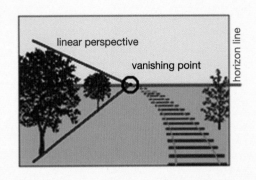

surface. It can make viewers feel as if they are looking at a scene through an open window.

In pictures with linear perspective, a viewer can find the horizon line and vanishing point. The horizon is where the sky meets the ground. The vanishing point is near the center of the horizon line.

1. What is the place where the sky meets the ground in the paintings?
   a. Linear perspective
   b. Horizon line
   c. Vanishing point
   d. Illusion

2. All of the following are true about linear perspective except
   a. A technique used in painting
   b. A technique for creating realistic picture
   c. A technique for looking out a window
   d. A technique for creating an illusion of distance on a flat surface

IV **Read the passage and answer questions.**

There were important changes in style in ancient Egyptian paintings. In the Old Kingdom, the pictures were almost always about daily lives. But in the New Kingdom, there were pictures about events or a big battle that happened. In addition, the paintings were expressed in very dramatic and exaggerated ways in the New Kingdom.

After the Persians conquered Egypt, Egyptian art was influenced by different cultures such as Persian, Greek, Roman, and Islamic. Each of these cultures was mixed with Egyptian culture in a different way.

1. What can you see in the pictures of the Old Kingdom of Egypt?
   a. Important events
   b. Egyptians' daily lives.
   c. Dramatic stories
   d. Battle scenes

2. Which of the following does not influence Egyptian art?
   a. Persian culture
   b. Greek culture
   c. Roman culture
   d. Turkish culture

V   Read the passage and answer questions.

Vincent Van Gogh is undoubtedly one of the great artists in modern art. He was a gifted artist but he lived a sad and hard life. In general, he did not feel secure about his life and he was confused with himself and outer world.

Van Gogh took some medicine called Fox Glove to relieve his uneasiness. But the medicine sometimes made him lose his temper. Once he got so mad and depressed, he cut off his own ear. He did not find happiness with any woman. He finished his life by committing suicide one day in July of 1890.

1. **Why did Van Gogh take the medicine called Fox Glove?**
   a. Because he had a stomachache.
   b. Because he wanted to draw a great painting.
   c. Because he lost his tempe.
   d. Because he wanted to relieve his uneasiness.

2. **Which of the following is not true about Van Gogh?**
   a. He was an artist.
   b. He married the woman he loved.
   c. He felt insecure about his life.
   d. He killed himself.

Actual Mini *TOEFL*

Read the paragraph and answer questions.

Many of Picasso's pictures may look strange. This is because Picasso showed many different views of person or an object at the same time. *He* drew the front and the side of a face in the same picture. His artistic style is called cubism.

In the early 20th century in Europe, many artists were turning away from traditional painting and were struggling to ***produce*** more innovative and unique works. For some of them, innovation itself was a goal. This trend greatly influenced Picasso. Picasso created a new art movement called cubism. Many critics and viewers often misunderstood early cubist paintings. However, the cubist movement in paintings had a major influence on Western art and artists.

1. **What is the main topic of the passage?**
   a. Picasso's life
   b. Picasso's works
   c. Picasso's cubism
   d. Picasso's museum

2. **The word "He" in the passage refers to**

    a. European

    b. Picasso

    c. Artist of the early 20th century

    d. Cubist

3. **The word "produce" in the passage is closest in meaning to**

    a. print

    b. copy

    c. draw

    d. move

4. **What is the word that represents Picasso's artistic style?**

    a. Cubism

    b. Realism

    c. Naturalism

    d. Modernism

5. **Which of the following is not true about the cubist movement?**

    a. Many viewers misunderstood early cubist painting.

    b. The movement influenced on Western art.

    c. Picasso created the movement.

    d. Many artists tried to produce traditional paintings.

11

The Ancient Culture

11 The Ancient Culture

A. Arrange the following Sentences in order.

a. People started to trade for what they needed.

b. Long ago, most people ate and wrote what they could produce.

c. Today people buy and sell the things on Internet.

d. They used money to trade things.

_____

B. Choose the Sentences that comes in the blanks and write it.

Clothing was expensive in ancient times. It was very hard to make clothes by hand. _____. Many children had no clothes at all.

a. People started to use machines to make clothes.

b. Most people had very few clothes.

c. People bought their clothes at a store.

II

In ancient China rice was the first crop that was farmed. Rice farming traces back to about 5,000B.C. In northern China, wheat was a major crop, while in southern China it was mostly rice. (A) There was  a lot of trade between China and the West. (B) Chinese people mainly exported silk to the West and imported gold. (C) Some of the traders went to south to India, and some went Persia along the Silk Road. (D) By about 1,100 A.D. people began to use paper money in China.

1. The following sentences can be added to the passage.

   Bronze Coins *were used in China by 400 B.C.*

   Where would it best fit in the passage?

2. All of the following are true about ancient China EXCEPT
   a. People did not eat wheat.
   b. People used silk.
   c. Traders traveled to the West.
   d. China imported gold.

III

Before the Americas were discovered by Columbus, there lived many different groups of people with cultures in the land. Some of the more famous of  these include the Maya and the Inca civilization.

The Mayan civilization is one of the best-known civilizations that existed in the Americas. (A) The Mayans worshiped gods and built temples and palaces. (B) They developed astronomy, numbers, and their own calendar. (C) Some of these accomplishments were forgotten or destroyed as Spain conquered in the sixteenth century. (D) The remains show their lives and cultures.

1. The following sentences can be added to the passage.

   However, some of them were not destroyed.

2. Which of the following is not true about the Mayans in Americas?
   a. They knew how to build temples.
   b. They had a very advanced culture.
   c. They were not interested in stars.
   d. They used calendars.

Actual Mini *TOEFL*

Food is an essential part of culture. (A) The food people ate in ancient times was different from time to time and place to place.

(B) First, there was no refrigerator. (C) It was very hard to keep food fresh for a long time. (D) This made people think of various ways to *preserve* food. They dried or pickled fruit, vegetables, and meat. They made wine, cider, and beer. They smoked meat and made ham and bacon.

Second, people could only eat what they farmed in their area. If the weather was bad, people starved because of a shortage of food. People did not know many of today's foods. Potatoes, tomatoes, and corn didn't even exist until America was discovered.

1. **What is the main topic of the passage?**
   a. Ways to keep food fresh
   b. Various foods people eat
   c. New kinds of food
   d. The food in ancient times

2. The following sentence can be added to the passage.

    However, there was something they had in commons.

3. The word "preserve" in the passage is closest in meaning to
    a. promise
    b. keep
    c. cook
    d. invent

4. Which of the following is not mentioned as a way to preserve food?

   a. Drying

   b. Boiling

   c. Pickling

   d. Smoking

5. According to the passage, when did Europeans eat potatoes

   a. Before the 1st Century

   b. Around the 11th Century

   c. After trading with China

   d. After America was discovered

12

Weather Forecast

12 Weather Forecast

A. Choose the fact that can be inferred from the passage.

A meteorologist is a person who studies the earth's atmosphere to predict weather conditions. Meteorologists use technology to predict the weather. They use radar, satellite images, and lightning detectors to forecast different types of weather.

a. Meteorologists invented radar.
b. Radar helps forecast a tornado.

B. Read the passage and draw O if the following statements can be inferred and draw X if they cannot.

Weather forecasts give people information about the weather to come. In severe weather situations like hurricanes, forecast can help save lives and protect buildings. Weather forecasts should be accurate because so many people depend upon them.

a. Only severe weather is informed first. ____
b. People listen to weather forecasts when there is going to be a hurricane. ____
c. Many people expect accurate weather forecasts. ____
d. Weather forecasts are always accurate. ____

II

Radar is an important tool for weather forecasting. It detects the nature of a remote object by means of radio waves reflected from the object. Since the development of radar system, weather has become less mysterious. Long ago, people blamed gods for sudden and violent weather changes. Today radar makes it possible to predict violent weather.

Radar was invented through the principle of radio waves. In 1887, Heinrich Hertz began experimenting with radio waves in his laboratory in German. Hertz's experiments were the basis for the development of radar.

1. Which of the following can be inferred from the passage?
   a. Radar prevents heavy rainfall.
   b. Heinrich Hertz helped forecast weather.
   c. Radar is used in many experiments.
   d. Germany has the best weather forecasting system.

2. How does radar detect the nature of a remote object?
   a. By the shape of the object
   b. By the colour of the object
   c. By means of experiment
   d. By means of radio waves reflected from the object

III

Meteorological satellites made weather forecasting more scientific and correct. It gives people information about the climate on the earth.

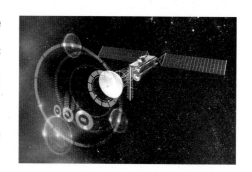

In 1960, the first weather satellite called Tiros started orbiting the earth. It carried a video camera and observed the earth regularly. For the first time, scientists were able to compare their ground-based weather observations with broader pictures from the weather system. Next, the Nimbus series moved in a polar orbit. After these satellites, more weather satellites were put into orbit to send weather data and pictures.

1. It can be inferred from the passage that
   a. today's weather satellites do not have video cameras.
   b. weather satellites can orbit the sun.
   c. today, many weather satellites orbit the earth.
   d. satellites sometimes send incorrect weather data.

2. What made weather forecasting more correct?
   a. Video cameras
   b. Meteorological satellites
   c. Pictures
   d. Ground-based observations

IV

Clouds are formed by the upward moving of air. As air rises, the moisture in the rising air cools and forms clouds. Moisture in clouds becomes water drops and the drops make clouds heavier. As  the clouds grow in size, the water drops begin to fall back to the earth. This cause rain or snow.

Active and dynamic air movement causes heavy clouds and can make heavy rains and powerful thunderstorms. If the air is quite humid and there is wind, it is likely to rain or snow.

1. **It can be inferred from the passage that**
   a. heavy rains make heavy clouds.
   b. without air movement, there is no rain.
   c. rising air makes clouds lighter.
   d. rising air dries moisture in clouds.

2. **What does active air movement make?**
   a. Moisture
   b. Clear sky
   c. Warm weather
   d. A thunderstorm

Actual Mini TOEFL

When forecasting temperature, people may *watch* clouds in the sky. During the daytime, the earth is heated by the sun. If the sky is clear, more heat reaches the earth's surface. This causes the temperature to rise. However, if the sky is cloudy, only the small amount of the sun's energy is able to reach the earth's surface. This causes the earth to *heat* more slowly. This leads to low temperature.

At night, clouds have the opposite effect. If the sky is clear, the heat on the earth's surface easily cools and this makes the temperature drop. However, if clouds cover the sky, higher temperatures are expected. Clouds prevent the heat on the earth's surface from being released and keep the earth warm.

1. **What is the main topic of the passage?**
   a. Forecasting rainfall
   b. Forecasting violent weather
   c. Forecasting temperature
   d. Forecasting cloudy days

2. According to the passage, what does a clear night say about the weather?

    a. It will be warmer.

    b. It will be cooler.

    c. It will snow.

    d. It will rain.

3. The word "heat" in the passage is opposite in meaning to

    a. cool

    b. boil

    c. freeze

    d. melt

4. Which of the following can be inferred from the passage?

    a. Clouds block the heat from the sun at night.

    b. Clouds keep the heat on the earth at night.

    c. During the day, clouds cause the rain.

    d. During the day, only a clear sky is expected.

5. The word "watch" in the passage is closest in meaning to

    a. draw

    b. discover

    c. experiment

    d. observe

13
Craft

13 Craft

A. Choose the fact that can be inferred from the passage.

A puppet is any character controlled by strings, sticks or by the use of a glove. There are hand puppets, stick puppets, and string puppets. The string puppet is called a marionette. It was a puppet character in the puppet plays of the Middle Ages.

a. String puppets have been used since the Middle Ages.
b. Stick puppets are names of characters in a puppet play.

B. Read the passage and draw O if the following statements can be inferred and draw X if they cannot.

A quilter chooses a pattern and cuts pieces of cloth. Then the quilter stitches them together to form an overall design. Once the top layer is as big as the quilter wants, it's joined together with the filling and the bottom layer.

a. Quilter knows how to stitch. ____

b. A quilt is made of pieces of cloth. ____

c. The top layer is bigger than the bottom layer. ____

d. Cloth is cut out as the quilter wants. ____

II

Masks have been made from various materials and for many purposes. Who made the first masks or even when or why is not exactly known. Some people believe men wore masks to hide themselves while hunting. Others think people made masks to frighten their enemy on the battlefield.

Some cultures believe that the person wearing a mask will have the character of the mask. The Pacific Northwest Indians wore great bird masks to have fierce spirits like the birds.

1. **Which of the following can be inferred from the passage?**
   a. Many types of masks exist.
   b. People usually wear scary masks.
   c. Hunters still wear masks today.
   d. Masks were developed only near the ocean.

2. **Why did the Pacific Northwest Indians wear masks?**
   a. To show their belief in the power of nature
   b. To have the character of the mask
   c. To hide themselves
   d. To frighten their enemy

III

Pottery is the art of making a pot out of clay. In the American state of Georgia, making pottery has a long history. The red clay of north Georgian soil is very suitable for making pottery.

European who settled in Georgia during the 1700s made pottery. They produced pottery for practical use. They made plates, mugs, and jugs. Pottery became widespread in Georgia in the 1820s. The skills and techniques of making pottery have been passed onto other people. Several families still work to preserve the 200-year -old tradition of making pottery.

1. **Which of the following can be inferred from the passage?**
   a. Red clay does not fit for making pottery.
   b. Georgia pottery is not beautiful.
   c. Pottery was made in Georgia about 200 years ago.
   d. Europeans invented pottery.

2. **When did the pottery of Georgia become popular?**
   a. Before the Europeans arrived in Georgia
   b. In the 1700s
   c. In the 1820s
   d. In the 1950s

IV

People have enjoyed puppets for a very long time. The use of puppets dates back thousands of years. The first puppet may have been shadow puppets, which are mentioned in Greek philosophy.

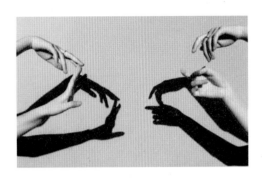

American Indians used spring puppets before the coming of Europeans. In Muslim countries, stories and legends were told through the shadow puppets. In the Middle Ages of Europe, puppets were used to give moral lessons. In the early 1800s in England, flat puppets along with their stage scenery were popular.

1. **It can be inferred from the passage that**

   a. puppet plays were moral in the Middle Ages of Europe.

   b. Europeans collected puppets in the Middle Ages.

   c. American Indians learned to make puppets from the Europeans.

   d. puppets started to be used after the 1st century.

2. **What kinds of puppets were used in the Muslim countries**

   a. String puppets

   b. Shadow puppets

   c. Flat puppets

   d. Finger puppets

Actual Mini *TOEFL*

A quilt can be compared to a sandwich. The two layers of cloth are the bread and the wool or cotton layer is the stuffing. All three layers are stitched together so the middle layer doesn't move around. These layers *trap* air and keep the person under quilt warm.

People all over the world have been quilting clothing and blankets for centuries. In America, quilts have been popular for generations. Patchwork quilting became very popular in the 19th century. When friends or family members left home, people made a quilt for *them* and stitched their names and wishes on the quilt. Quilting is not only for keeping warm, but also for decorating homes. Quilting is still popular in America today.

1. **What is the main topic of paragraph 2?**
   a. How to quilt
   b. Patterns of quilt
   c. Quilting in America
   d. The purpose of quilting

2. The word "them" in the passage refers to

   a. quilts

   b. Americans

   c. friends or family members

   d. names and wishes

3. The word "trap" in the passage is closest in meaning to

   a. trick

   b. treat

   c. clean

   d. catch

4. What can be inferred from the passage?

   a. Asians have been quilting.

   b. All Americans like quilting.

   c. Quilting is still very popular all over the world.

   d. A quilt is something to eat.

5. How many layers is a quilt made of?

   a. Two

   b. Three

   c. Four

   d. More than five

14

Poets and Novelists

14 Poets and Novelists

I

A. Arrange the following Sentences in order.

a. It was founded in 1900 according to his will.

b. Alfred Nobel invented dynamite.

c. He wanted to establish the Nobel Prize.

d. He earned a lot of money.

_____

B. Choose the sentence that comes in the blanks and write it.

Romeo and Juliet was written by William Shakespeare. Romeo and Juliet were deeply in love. _____.
Romeo saw Juliet sleeping and thought that she was dead, so he killed himself. When Juliet woke up and saw him dead, she killed herself too.

a. But their families were enemies.

b. They married at the end.

c. They were killed by their enemies.

II

Robert Frost is one of the greatest poets in American literature. __(A) In 1912, at the age of 38, he sold his farm and left for England, where he hoped to focus on writing poems. __(B) The book brought him to the attention of many critics.

Frost wrote about traditional farm life such as apple picking, fence, and country roads. __(C) He was fond of writing about rural subjects with everyday speech. __(D) His poems look simple but they suggest deeper meaning.

1. The following sentences can be added to the passage

   In London, he published his first book, A Boy's Will, in 1913.

   Where would it be best fit in the passage?
   Click on the underline to add the sentence to the passage.

2. Robert Frost wrote about all of the following EXCEPT
   a. farmers who pick apples
   b. fences with roads
   c. country roads
   d. hungry people in the city

III

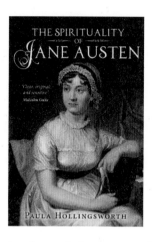

A British Novelist Jane Austen lived from 1775 to 1817. She was the seventh child out of eight. She was educated in her family. ___ (A) Within her family, she learned drawing and the piano. ___(B) She wrote that she and her family were "great novel readers." ___(C) In her twenties, she began to write her major novels.

___(D) Jane Austen is well-known for her wit and social observations. She wrote mainly about young, unmarried upper-class English women in the early 1800s. She left us with six major novels. Her novels have become more famous over time, and now she is known as one of the greatest English novelists.

1. The following sentences can be added to the passage.

   *One of them is **Pride and Prejudice**.*

2. What were Jane Austen's novels typically about?
   a. Young men in the 1700s
   b. Poor English people
   c. Unmarried women in the 1800s
   d. Workers and farmers

IV

Homer was a Greek poet. He lived around 700 B.C. It is believed that he was blind. ___(A) Homer wrote two long epic poems called the *Iliad* and the *Odyssey*. ___ (B) He didn't make up these stories. ___ (C) *The Odyssey* is the story of King Odysseus. It is about his return from the Trojan War to his kingdom.

___ (D) Homer's poems played a very important role to the Greeks. Students memorized Homer's writings in schools, and they repeated parts of it. They used it in persuading other people to do something or think about something.

1. The following sentence can be added to the passage.

   These stories had already been for hundreds of years.

2. What is *the Odyssey* mainly about?
   a. Greek people
   b. A Greek poet
   c. King Odysseus
   d. Homer's life

Actual Mini *TOEFL*

Ernest Hemingway's adventurous life helped him write novels. Hemingway spent his childhood in Michigan on hunting and fishing trips. ___(A) He volunteered for an ambulance unit in France during World War I, but he was ***wounded*** and stayed in a hospital for six months. ___(B) After he became famous as a novelist, he joined

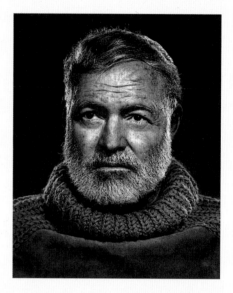

some other wars. ___ (C) On a safari in Africa, he was badly injured when his small plane crashed.

___ (D) He won the Pulitzer in 1953 with his novel, *The Old man and the Sea*. The next year, he ***earned*** the Nobel Prize. When he got old, he was troubled by family and illness. He finished his life by shooting himself.

1. **What is the main topic of the passage?**
   a. Hemingway's works
   b. Hemingway's adventurous life
   c. Hemingway's friends
   d. Hemingway's poor death

2. The following sentence can be added to the passage.

   After the war, in Paris, he met some American writers who influenced his writing style.

3. The word "wounded" in the passage is closest in meaning to
   a. locked
   b. caught
   c. injured
   d. hit

4. The word "earned" in the passage is OPPOSITE in meaning to
   a. won
   b. made
   c. lost
   d. spent

5. According to the passage, what gave Hemingway the Pulitzer Prize?
   a. His novel
   b. His poem
   c. His life
   d. His time in wars

15

Ecosystem

15 Ecosystem

I

A. Arrange the following Sentences in order.

a. Plants depend on sunlight and water.

b. Fish depend on frogs.

c. Frogs depend on these insects for food.

d. Insects and small animals depend on plants.

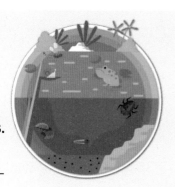

_____

B. Choose the sentences that comes in the blanks and write it.

In the summer, mosquitoes are the most common animals found in the lake. Only female mosquitoes suck blood. _____ _____. Male mosquitoes feed on plant nectar. Lizards, snakes, fish, dragonflies, and birds all feed on mosquitoes.

a. They cannot survive the winter.

b. Mosquitoes live in group.

c. Rabbits, birds, and other animals supply the blood.

II

Many kinds of plants and animals live throughout the world. They live in different places. However, all plants and animals live in ecosystems. An ecosystem is made up of living things and the environment they live in.

___ (A) All the parts of an ecosystem affect each other, whether they are living or nonliving. ___ (B) In a forest, leaves fall from trees and small insects break them down. ___ (C) In a pond, insects and small animals become food for frogs. ___(D) Grown frogs become food for fish.

1. The following sentence can be added to the passage.

   The broken leaves become the soil for trees.

2. What is an ecosystem made up of?
   a. Plants and animals
   b. Forests and ponds
   c. Animals and their food
   d. Living things and the environment

III

There is a law of the jungle. That means the strong survive through competition. All living things compete for space, water, food, or some other need. ___ (A) Grass-eating animals like zebras on the savanna compete for grass. ___ (B) Predators like lions also compete for prey.

___ (C) How about the plant kingdom? ___ (D) Plants in a forest compete for sunlight as well.

In nature, living things find ways to live in harmony. When various living things share the same ecosystem, they find different places and food to avoid competing.

1. The following sentence can be added to the passage.

If there is not enough grass, some zebras will not survive.

2. What do the plants in a forest compete for?
   a. Water
   b. Sunlight
   c. Food
   d. Prey

IV

The tundra is a cold plain. The soil in the tundra is permanently frozen. However, the tundra is actually home to many living things.

One tundra ecosystem is the Artic Costal Plain, where many animals have their homes. ___(A) There are wolves, artic foxes, polar bears, and hawks. Seals and walruses can be found in the water. ___(B) Different kinds of grasses and mosses make up the plant life. ___(C) Some colorful flowers bloom during the short summer. ___(D) Together, these plants and animals compose the Artic Coastal Plain ecosystem.

1. The following sentence can be added to the passage.

   But trees can hardly survive in the tundra.

2. Which of the following is NOT found on the Artic Coastal Plain?
   a. Animals like wolves
   b. Birds like hawks
   c. Colorful flowers
   d. Tall trees

Actual Mini *TOEFL*

There is a place in the United States called "River of Grass." The place got its name because of the thick grass that grows in the wet area. It is the Everglades in Florida. The Everglades is an  ecosystem which has hundreds of different living and nonliving things. The living and nonliving things affect each other.

Limestone is a nonliving part of the Everglades ecosystem. ___ (A) Water remains in these holes. ___(B) Plants grow in and around holes. ___(C) During the _dry_ season, fish, turtles, and other animals move into the holes for food. ___(D) The alligators feed on the fish, frogs, turtles, and other animals that have made their homes in the holes. Other nonliving things like hurricanes, drought, and lightening help keep an ecosystem in balance.

1. **What is the main topic of the passage?**
   a. The Everglades in Florida
   b. Nonliving parts of ecosystem
   c. The Everglades ecosystem
   d. The balance in a forest

2. The following sentence can be added to the passage.

   Alligators make holes in the limestone.

3. The word "dry" in the passage is OPPOSITE in meaning to
   a. hot
   b. sunny
   c. humid
   d. snowy

4. What is an example of nonliving things in an ecosystem?
   a. Lightening
   b. Trees
   c. Frogs
   d. Plants

5. Why do turtles move into the holes that alligators make?
   a. To sleep
   b. To find food
   c. To play with other turtles
   d. To eat alligators

신봉수

Temple University, 고려대학교 [문학박사, 영어교수법(TESOL) 전공]

(전) 고려대학교, 한국교원대학교, 충남대학교 시간강사
(전) 위덕대학교 영문과 교수
(전) 위덕대학교 입학, 학생처장

Senior Researcher & Visiting Professor
at Bilingual Research Centre of McMaster University (Canada)

저서: 영어교육입문 (서울: 박영사)
　　　영어교육의 이론과 실제 (위덕대학교 출판부)

McMaster English _ Intermediate Reading

초판1쇄 인쇄　2019년　5월　10일
초판1쇄 발행　2019년　5월　15일

편저자　　신 봉 수
펴낸이　　임 순 재

펴낸곳　　(주)한올출판사
등 록　　제11-403호
주 소　　서울시 마포구 모래내로 83(성산동, 한올빌딩 3층)
전 화　　(02)376-4298(대표)
팩 스　　(02)302-8073
홈페이지　www.hanol.co.kr
e-메일　　hanol@hanol.co.kr

ISBN 979-11-5685-772-3